ALBANY COUNTY
PUBLIC LIBRARY
Serving the Laramie Plains since 1887

Laramie, Wyoming 82070

PRESENTED BY

Friends of the Library

GRANDMA SUSAN REMEMBERS

Library of Congress Cataloging-in-Publication Data

Morris, Ann, 1930-

Grandma Susan remembers: a British-American family story/Ann Morris;

photographs and illustrations by Peter Linenthal.

p. cm. — (What was it like, grandma?)

ISBN 0-7613-2319-8 (lib. bdg.)

1. British Americans—Maine—Social life and customs—Juvenile literature.
2. Family—Maine—Juvenile literature. 3. Grandmothers—Maine—Juvenile
literature. 4. Southwest Harbor (Me. : Town)—Social life and customs—
Juvenile literature. I. Linenthal, Peter. II. Title.

F30.B7 M67 2002   974.1—dc21   2001044614

The Millbrook Press, Inc.

2 Old New Milford Road

Brookfield, Connecticut 06804

www.millbrookpress.com

What Was It Like, Grandma?

GRANDMA SUSAN REMEMBERS

A British-American Family Story

Ann Morris

Photographs and illustrations by Peter Linenthal

The Millbrook Press

Brookfield, Connecticut

Southwest Harbor, Maine

On the rocky coast of Maine is a small fishing village called Southwest Harbor. It's an old-fashioned town with one main street. At the end of the street is a harbor for fishing boats and pleasure boats.

It gets crowded in Southwest Harbor during the summer. That's when people come to enjoy the fishing and boating.

Gordon, Sarah, and Susan visit the village often.

Their grandparents Susan and Jarvis live here with their cat, Bandit.

Gordon, Sarah, and Susan with Grandma Susan and Bandit

The three children live more than a hundred miles away in Woolwich, Maine, with their mother and father, Kathe and Robert. But they spend a lot of time with their grandmother and grandfather. From their grandparents' big brick house, you can hear the foghorns warning boats to stay away from the rocky shore.

The children call Grandma Susan "Nana."

When they visit, they share in many of the interesting things she does — gardening, sewing, cooking, and reading.

Often they go to the library with Nana. They have family reading times at night. Gordon loves to have Nana read his favorite book, *Tikki Tikki Tembo*, over and over.

Grandma Susan makes teddy bears.

Imagine having a grandmother who is an expert teddy-bear maker!

The children like to watch her sew.

Of course, Gordon, Susan, and Sarah have their own special bears to play with.

Sometimes the children have parties for the bears. Sometimes Nana makes teddy-bear cookies for these parties.

A Teddy-Bear Party

A teddy-bear party can be lots of fun.

HERE ARE IDEAS FOR YOUR PARTY:

1. Bring your own bear.

2. Give the bears a special table of their own.

3. Serve cookies shaped like bears and glasses of lemonade.

4. Make bear pictures, games, or objects. For example, you could make bear key chains. Make the bears out of polymer modeling clay and paint. Then attach them to key chains.

The children love looking at old family pictures.

Grandma Susan and Grandpa Jarvis tell them what things were like when they were little.

Jarvis's family and Susan's family have lived in the area for many generations. Their ancestors were British. Grandpa Jarvis's father was a lobsterman and greatly loved the sea. He used traps made of wooden slats to catch the lobsters.

Grandpa Jarvis is proud of his seafaring family.

Grandpa Jarvis shows the children a model of one of the first *Friendship* sloops.

Grandpa Jarvis also loves the sea. He is a boatbuilder.

Jarvis builds *Friendship* sloops, old-fashioned sailboats with one mast and three sails. These sloops were once used mainly for fishing. Now they are used for fun and for racing.

Some *Friendship* sloops are made out of wood. But Jarvis makes most of his out of sturdy fiberglass.

Jarvis also builds Maine powerboats. These boats can go very fast.

There are many islands near Southwest Harbor. When Grandma Susan was very little, she lived on Cranberry Island, but her family soon moved to Southwest Harbor.

Susan has one older sister, Ann, and two younger brothers, Raymond and James.

She remembers the fun she had playing with them when she was growing up.

Grandma Susan
(about age four) dressed
for winter

Susan's brothers—
James (age two) and
Raymond (age four)

Ann (age sixteen)
and Susan (age
thirteen)

One of the boats Raymond built

Raymond working in his shop

Grandma Susan's father, Great-grandpa Raymond, was also a boatbuilder.

His shop was in Southwest Harbor. He built Maine-style lobster boats from cedar and oak. He also made pleasure boats.

Young Susan at the beach

with her mother

Grandma Susan's family used to take boat rides to places where they could picnic, swim, hike, or camp.

Grandma Susan's high school
graduation picture

Grandma Susan was a very good student.

After high school she went to school to learn to be a secretary.

Susan and Jarvis attended the same church and the same school. Jarvis is several years older than Susan, so they never met there. Later when they were both working in Boston, they did meet. They became good friends and within a year, he proposed to her—in a sailboat. Soon after, they married and began to have children.

Nana takes her grandchildren on a short boat ride to Cranberry Island, her childhood home.

She tells them how much she still loves Cranberry Island and visiting the home where she first lived. "Every Father's Day we had a picnic on the beach at Little Cranberry Island," she tells Gordon, Sarah, and Susan.

The children also love Cranberry Island.

They play on the wide lawns around the house and pick blueberries.

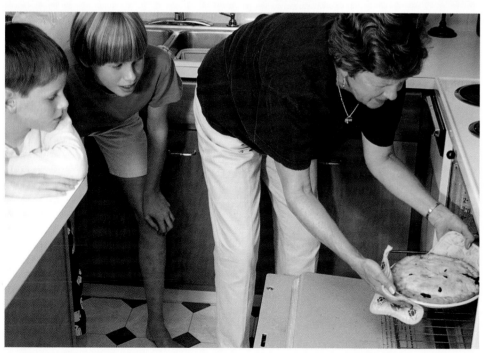

After an afternoon of berry picking, the children help Nana make a blueberry pie.

She uses the same family recipe her mother used.

Blueberry Pie

SAFETY TIP:

If you try this recipe, get an adult to help.

HERE IS WHAT YOU NEED:

- 2 uncooked piecrusts, rolled out (use your own recipe)
- 4 cups blueberries, picked over and rinsed
- 1 cup sugar
- 2 tablespoons flour

Pinch salt

- 1/4 teaspoon ground nutmeg
- 1/4 teaspoon ground cinnamon
- 1 tablespoon lemon juice
- 1 tablespoon butter

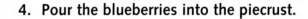

HERE IS WHAT YOU DO:

1. Line a 9-inch pie plate with one of the crusts.

2. Sprinkle the salt on the bottom of the piecrust.

3. In a bowl, mix the sugar and flour together. Spread 1/4 cup of the mixture on the bottom piecrust.

4. Pour the blueberries into the piecrust.

5. Sprinkle the remaining sugar-and-flour mixture onto the blueberries.

6. Sprinkle the nutmeg, cinnamon, and lemon juice over the berries. Dot with butter.

7. Place the second piecrust over the blueberry mixture. Use your fingers or a fork to press the piecrust tightly to the lower crust and the edge of the pie plate. Cut off the extra crust.

8. Make a few slits in the crust with a knife.

9. Bake 40 minutes at 425°F.

10. Remove from oven. Put the pie on a rack and let cool.

11. Top with vanilla ice cream and serve.

There are several lighthouses near Southwest Harbor.

When Nana was young, she and her mother went on special outings to the famous lighthouse at Duck Island.

During World War II, Nana's cousin used to be the lighthouse keeper there.
For many years the lighthouse guided ships coming into the harbor.

Now Nana shows the children another lighthouse—at Bass Harbor Head. It is a long hike to the lighthouse. The children climb over the rocks beneath the lighthouse and play on the beach. Gordon spots a boat. "Look, there's a sloop," he says.

When Nana was a little girl, many people in Maine made their living catching lobsters. Many still do. Nana's brother has been a lobster fisherman for thirty years.

Lobsters are a specialty of the area.

The whole Newman family loves lobsters. Sometimes they go down to Beal's Wharf in Southwest Harbor for lunch. Each child chooses a lobster. After they are cooked, Nana helps the children crack the lobsters open. What a feast!

Maybe one day, Gordon, Sarah, and Susan will teach their grandchildren how to make teddy bears and blueberry pies, catch lobsters, and sail all kinds of boats!

ALL ABOUT MY FAMILY

Would you like to know about your family? Here are some things you can do.

INTERVIEWS

You will find out many interesting things about your relatives by interviewing them. Ask them questions about their childhood—where they lived, what they liked best to do and to eat, what they read and studied in school. Find out, too, how things are different today from when they were young. Use a tape recorder to record your questions and their answers.

FAMILY ALBUM

Ask your relatives for pictures of themselves. Put all the pictures in an album. Write something you have learned about each person under his or her picture.

FAMILY TREE

All of us have many relatives. Some of us are born into the family. Others are related by marriage or have been adopted. You can make a family tree that looks like the one on the next page to show who belongs to your family.

NEWMAN FAMILY TREE

Susan

Jarvis

Kathe

Robert

Gordon

Sarah

Susan